ALSO BY
AOIFE DOOLEY

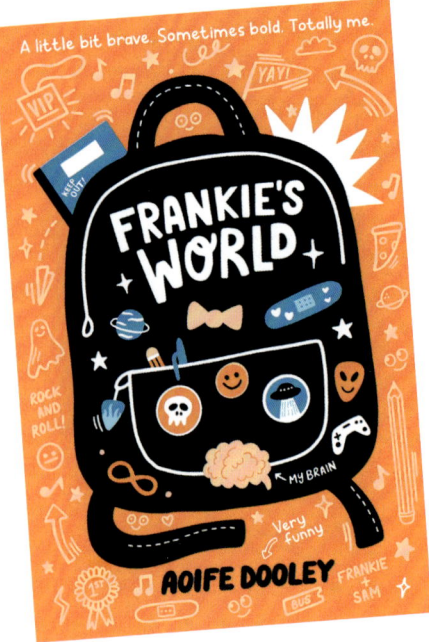

Frankie's World

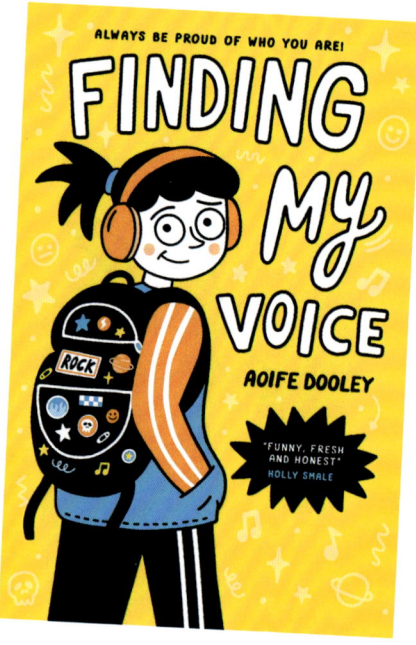

Finding My Voice

Published in the UK by Scholastic, 2025
Scholastic, Bosworth Avenue, Warwick, CV34 6UQ

SCHOLASTIC and associated logos are trademarks and/or
registered trademarks of Scholastic Inc.

Text and illustrations © Aoife Dooley, 2025

The moral rights of the author and illustrator have been asserted by them.

ISBN 978 0702 33710 9

A CIP catalogue record for this book is available from the British library.

All rights reserved.
This book is sold subject to the condition that it shall not, by way of
trade or otherwise, be lent, hired out or otherwise circulated in
any form of binding or cover other than that in which it is published.
No part of this publication may be reproduced, stored in a retrieval
system, or transmitted in any form or by any other means (electronic,
mechanical, photocopying, recording or otherwise) or used to train any
artificial intelligence technologies without prior written permission
of Scholastic limited. Subject to EU law Scholastic limited expressly
reserves this work from the text and data mining exception.

Printed in China
Paper made from wood grown in sustainable
forests and other controlled sources.

10 9 8 7 6 5 4 3 2 1

This is a work of fiction. Any resemblance to actual
people, events or locales is entirely coincidental.

www.scholastic.co.uk

For safety or quality concerns:
UK: www.scholastic.co.uk/productinformation
EU: www.scholastic.ie/productinformation

Contents

The Middle of Nowhere........... 1
Where's Barney?............... 22
What's That Noise?............. 89
Flushed Away 148

Welcome to NOWHERE

FUN FACTS

Ollie
Ollie is a vampire squid! He can turn himself inside out and glow in the dark. Did you know that vampire squids are real? They only grow to the size of a football and glow to escape other sea creatures.

Zing
Zing is a sea bunny, a type of sea slug. Sea slugs come in all different colours and can be toxic. Zings releases toxins when he gets anxious or scared, and they make his friends fall asleep!

Barney
Barney is a sea anemone and is Ollie and Zing's pet. Anemones spend most of their time attached to rocks and can live up to 100 years or more!

Thornelius

Thornelius is another type of sea slug and is toxic like his arch enemy, Zing. He can shoot thorns at other fish so he can escape sticky situations!

Hypno

Hypno is a type of sea snail who has the power to hypnotize other sea creatures. His shell creates an optical illusion leading other fish to become confused.

Sneaky

Sneaky is a shark. He is always popping up and trying to scare you. Did you know that sharks have been around for over 400 million years?

Ned

Ned is a flounder and runs the town's local knick-knack store. He's always trying to scam the other fish. Did you know that flounders have a flat body?

Aidan

Aidan is a boxfish and part of the local skater group. He can read the emotions of other sea creatures and tell when they are lying. Did you know that boxfish are slow swimmers due to their body shape?

Buck

Buck is another type of boxfish. Buck uses his hair to swim faster. He can see perfectly in the dark.

Liberty

Liberty is a sea urchin and is friends with Buck and Aidan. Did you know that urchins don't have any bones and there's a type of species called a sea potato?

Colette

Colette is an angler fish. They are known for their glowing 'fishing rods'. There are over 200 species of angler fish and they can camouflage themselves to hide from other creatures.

Michel
Michel is a crab and the town's local artist. He loves to paint in his gallery. His shell changes colour depending on what mood he is in.

The Blob
The Blob is the stinkiest sea creature in the ocean. Think about the worst smell ever and multiply by ten! He can release smells that last for months.

Gus
Gus is a jellyfish and runs the town's local bakery. Did you know that jellyfish are 95-98% water and their stings can be painful for humans?

Snakey is one of the most mysterious creatures in the ocean and has not yet been discovered by humans. Snakey can grow to up five times her usual size!

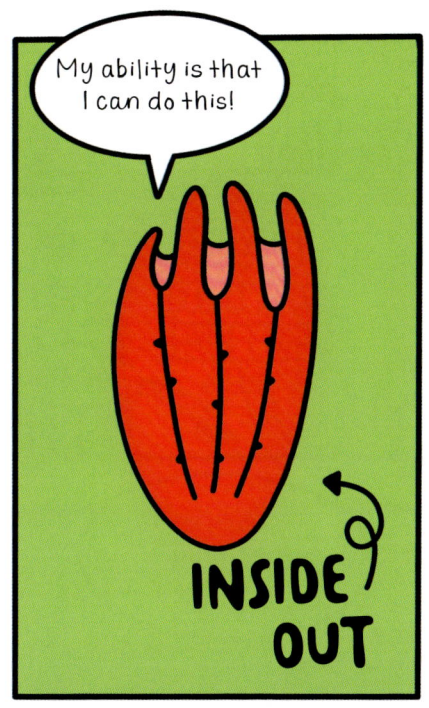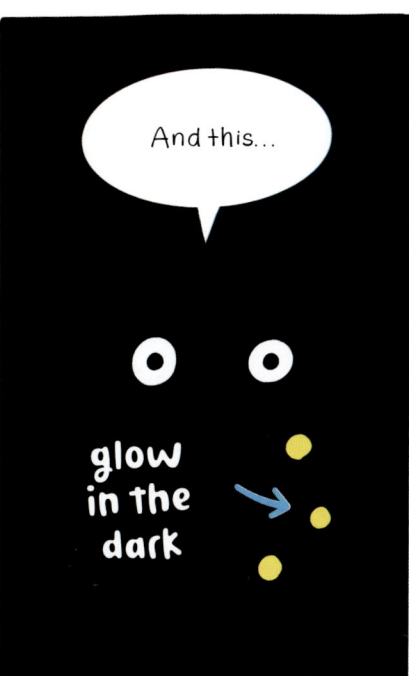

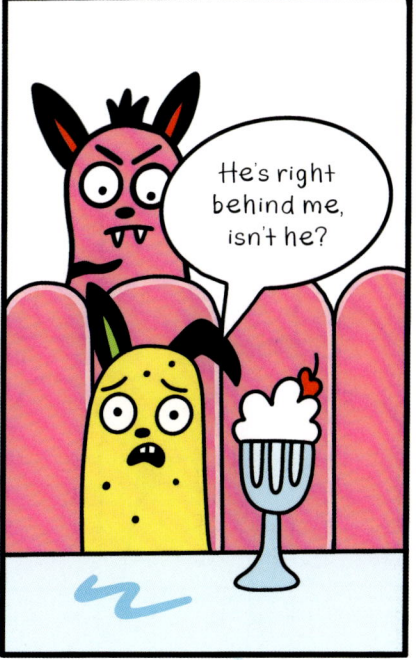

WHERE'S BARNEY?

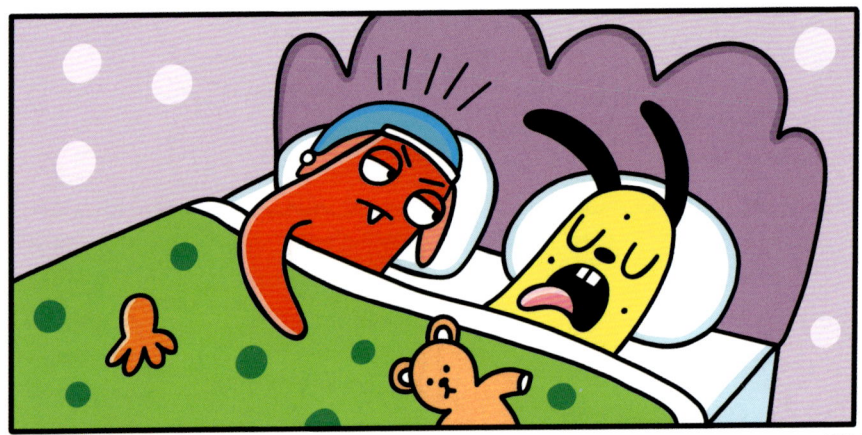

What's that noise?

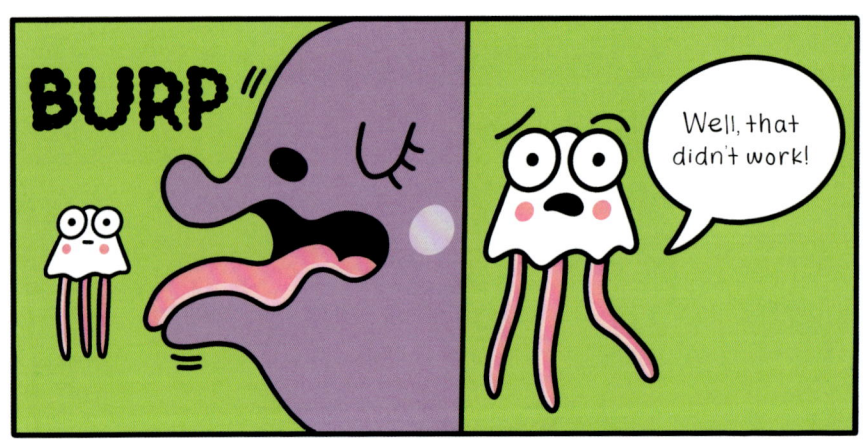

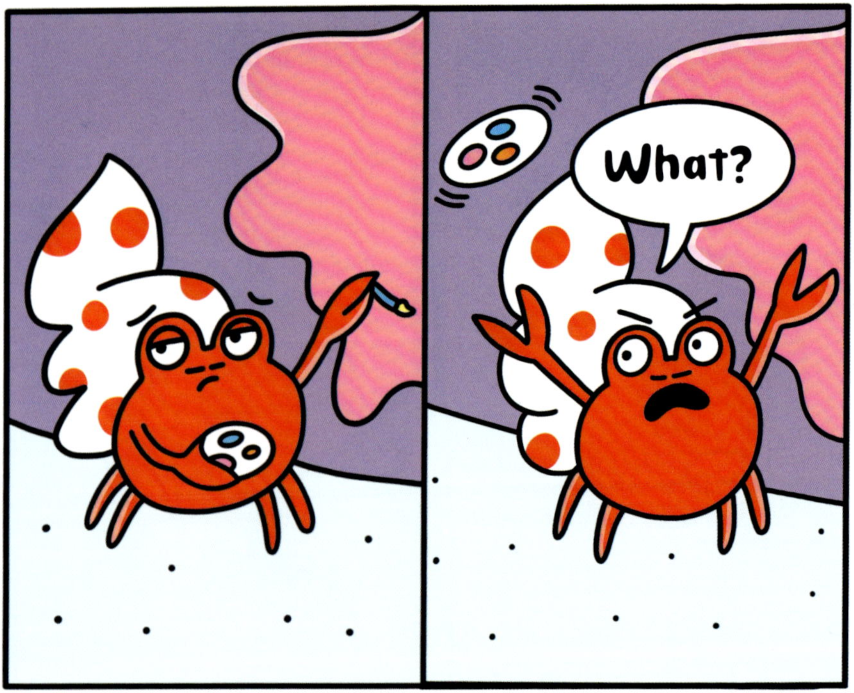

What?

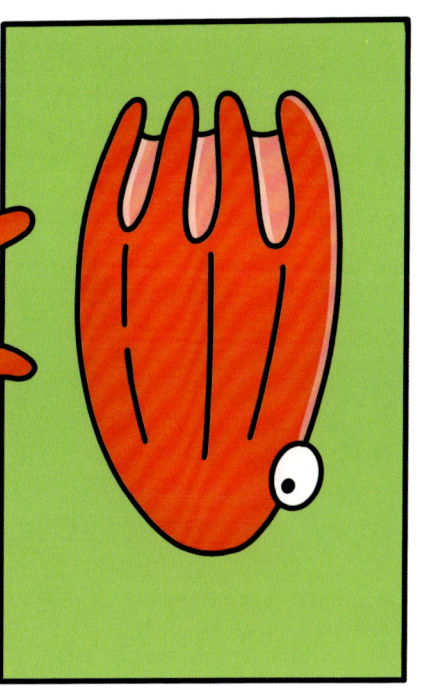

AHHHHHHHH!

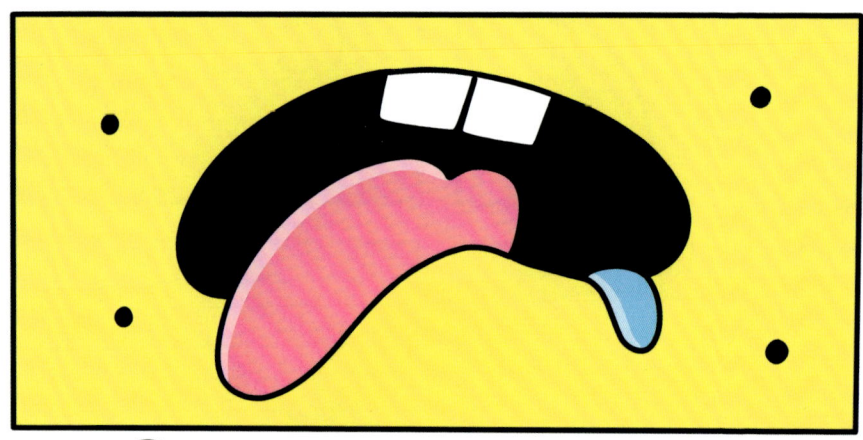

MEANWHILE...

Where's my sea-moss rug?! ZINNNNNNGGGGG!!!!

FLUSHED AWAY

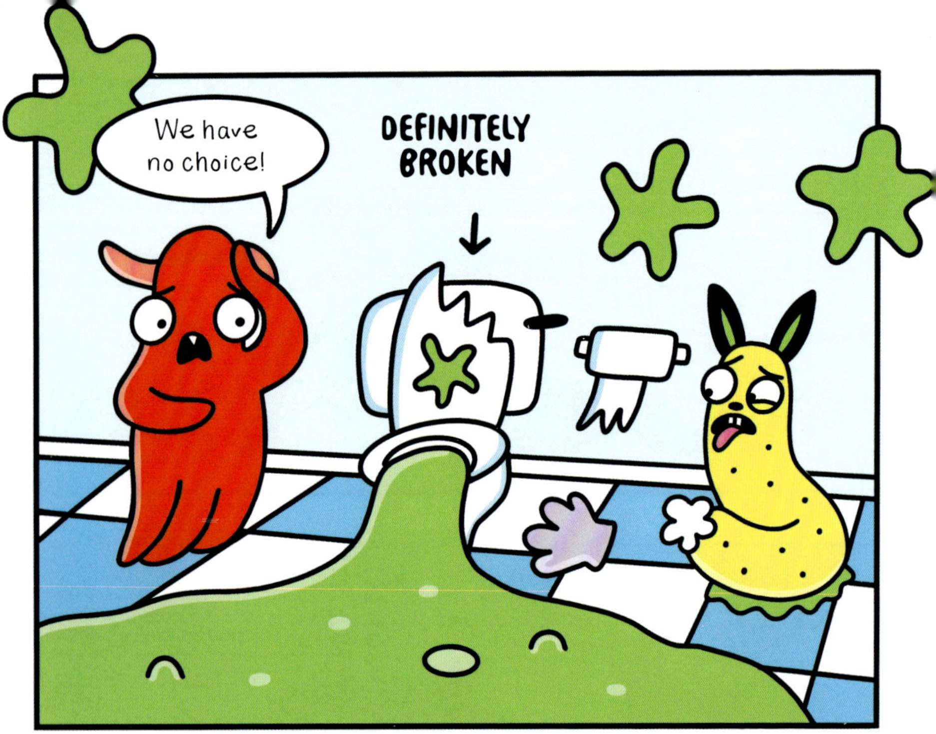

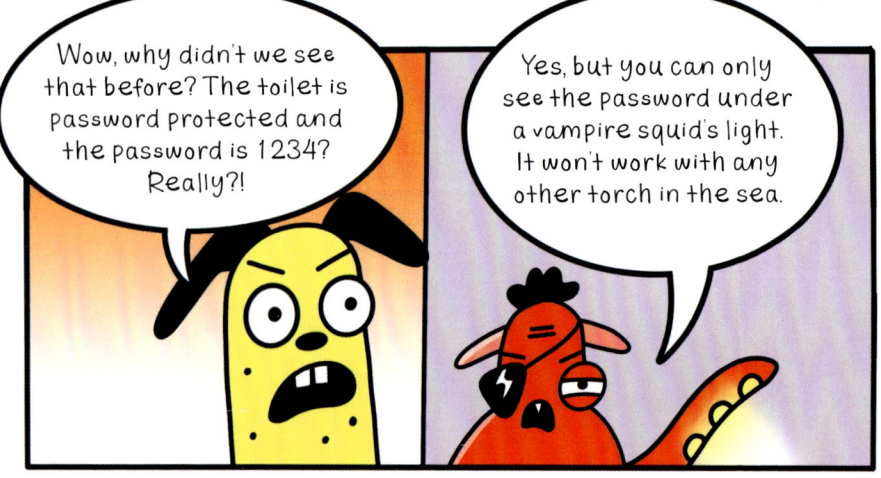

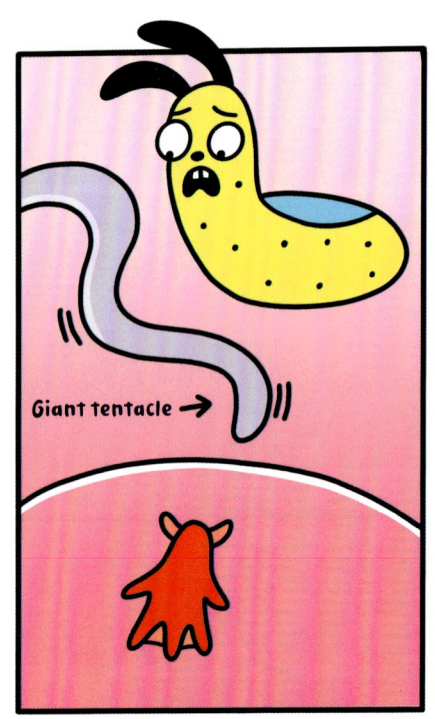

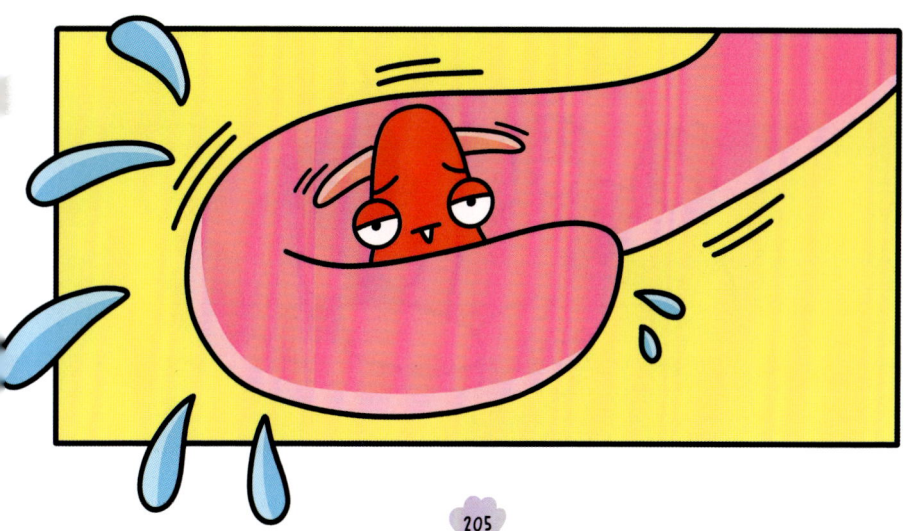

WHAT'S YOUR SEA NICKNAME?

Pick the month you were born and the first letter of your name to find out your funny sea nickname

Jan Danger	**A** Bubbles	**N** Starfish
Feb Mc Captain	**B** Barnacles	**O** Snapper
Mar Sir Crabby	**C** Unicorn Thing	**P** Sea Slug
Apr Mc Crusty	**D** Flounder	**Q** Seaweed
May Sir Breezy	**E** Blow Hole	**R** Sailor
Jun Mc Windy	**F** Shrimples	**S** Crab
Jul Mc Sluggy	**G** Shells	**T** Jelly
Aug Sir Wiggly	**H** Squiddy	**U** Whirlpool
Sep Mc Bubbly	**I** Scallop	**V** Paddle
Oct Mc Jelly	**J** Big Boat	**W** Sand
Nov Mc Dolphin	**K** Lagoon	**X** Tuna
Dec Mc Shippy	**L** Reef	**Y** Wave
	M Algae	**Z** Crustacean

Acknowledgments

I would like to thank my amazing editor, Julia Sanderson, for her support and encouragement throughout making Squid Squad and for making this adventure what it is. To my amazing agent, Faith O'Grady, thank you for your support for this book and beyond over the last 10 years. I would also like to thank all the team at Scholastic including Wendy Shakespeare, Sarah Dutton, Andrew Biscomb and Rachel Lawston for your amazing work and patience in making this book and bringing this story to life.

To booksellers, librarians, teachers, parents, SNAs thank you so much for your continued support and for introducing kids to a different way of reading when they feel like reading is not for them. You are making the world a better place and I can see it when I meet these kids at different events. You are amazing.

To my family and friends for your patience, love and support and for making this last year easier. You are legends.

ABOUT THE AUTHOR

AOIFE IS AN AWARD-WINNING AUTHOR, ILLUSTRATOR AND COMEDIAN FROM DUBLIN, IRELAND.

AOIFE OFTEN SHARES HER EXPERIENCES OF BEING DIAGNOSED AS AUTISTIC AT THE AGE OF 27 AND HOW A DIAGNOSIS HELPED HER TO TRULY UNDERSTAND HERSELF.